once upon a mattress

Music by
MARY RODGERS

Lyrics by
MARSHALL BARER

Book by
JAY THOMPSON, MARSHALL BARER *and* **DEAN FULLER**

Piano Reduction by Robert H. Noeltner

for this edition:
Musical Supervision by Bruce Pomahac
Musical Preparation by Scott Tilley

chappell/intersong
music group—usa

EXCLUSIVELY DISTRIBUTED BY

HAL•LEONARD®
CORPORATION
7777 W. BLUEMOUND RD. P.O. BOX 13819 MILWAUKEE, WI 53213

once upon a mattress

Produced by T. Edward Hambleton, Norris Houghton & William *and* Jean Eckart
First performance May 11, 1959 at the Phoenix Theater, New York City

Directed by GEORGE ABBOTT

Dances and Musical Numbers Staged by JOE LAYTON
Scenery and Costumes by WILLIAM and JEAN ECKART
Lighting by THARON MUSSER
Musical Direction by HAL HASTINGS
Orchestrations by HERSHY KAY, ARTHUR BECK *and* CARROLL HUXLEY
Dance Music Arranged by ROGER ADAMS

Cast of Characters
(In order of appearance)

Prologue

Minstrel	Harry Snow
Prince	Jim Maher
Princess	Chris Karner
Queen	Gloria Stevens

Wizard	Robert Weil
Princess Number Twelve	Mary Stanton
Lady Rowena	Dorothy Aull
Lady Merrill	Patsi King
Prince Dauntless the Drab	Joe Bova
Queen Aggravain	Jane White
Lady Lucille	Luce Ennis
Lady Larken	Anne Jones
Sir Studley	Jerry Newby
King Sextimus the Silent	Jack Gilford
Jester	Matt Mattox
Sir Harry	Allen Case
Princess Winnifred	Carol Burnett
Sir Harold	David Neuman
Lady Beatrice	Gloria Stevens
Sir Luce	Tom Mixon
Lady Mabelle	Chris Karner
The Nightingale of Samarkand	Ginny Perlowin
Lady Dorothy	Dorothy D'Honau
Sir Christopher	Christopher Edwards
Lord Howard	Howard Parker
Lady Dora	Dorothy Frank
Sir Daniel	Dan Resin
Sir Steven	Jim Stevenson
Lord Patrick	Julian Patrick

once upon a mattress

Synopsis of Scenes

The Time: *Many Moons Ago*
Place: *In and About a Medieval Castle*

ACT I

Scene 1: The Throne Room - late March
Scene 2: A Corridor - later that day
Scene 3: The Courtyard - a mid-April morning three weeks later
Scene 4: A Corridor - later that day
Scene 5: Princess Winnifred's Dressing Chamber - later that day
Scene 6: A Corridor - later that day
Scene 7: The Courtyard - late that evening
Scene 8: A Corridor- a few minutes later
Scene 9: The Great Hall - immediately following

ACT II

Scene 1: The Castle - that evening
Scene 2: Princes Winnifred's Dressing Chamber - later that evening
Scene 3: A Corridor - later that evening
Scene 4: The Wizard's Chamber - later that evening
Scene 5: A Corridor - immediately following
Scene 6: Another Corridor - three o'clock in the morning
Scene 7: Princess Winnifred's Bed Chamber - immediately following
Scene 8: A Corridor - the next morning
Scene 9: The Banquet Hall - at breakfast that morning

Orchestration

Flute (doubling Piccolo)	Guitar
Oboe	Percussion
Clarinet	Harp
Bass Clarinet	Piano (doubling Celeste)
French Horn	Violins
Trumpet I	Violas
Trumpet II	Cellos
Trombone	Bass

once upon a mattress

Musical Numbers

ONCE UPON A MATTRESS

Lyrics by
MARSHALL BARER

Music by
MARY RODGERS

Overture

Moderato

Segue as 1

No. 2

Prologue—Many Moons Ago

find a lass Who would suit his moth-er's pride. For a

18

prin-cess is a del-i-cate thing, Del-i-cate and dain-ty as a

dra-gon fly's wing. You can re-cog-nize a la-dy by her el-e-gant air, But a

24   26 *Keep moving*

gen-u-ine prin-cess is ex-ceed-ing-ly rare.

On a storm-y night, to the cas-tle door, Came the lass the prince had been wait-ing for. "I'm a prin-cess lost" quoth she. But the queen was cool and re-mained a-loof And she said: "Per-haps, but she'll need some proof. I'll pre-pare a test and see. I will

42

test her thus," the old queen said: I'll put twen-ty down-y mat-tress-

Hp.

+Tpt.
(Cls., Hns.
sust.)

Bs. pizz.

es up-on her bed And be-tween those twen-ty mat-tress-es I'll place a ti-ny pea. If that

(cont.)

(Hp.)

+Vlns.

Vla., Cl.

50 *a tempo*

pea dis-turbs her slum-ber, then a true prin-cess is she.

W.W.

Bell, Hp.

+Tpt.,
Str.

mf

+Hp.

Bells

Bells

Now, the bed was soft and ex-treme-ly tall, But the dain-ty lass did-n't sleep at all, And she told them so next day. Said the queen: "My dear, if you felt that pea, Then we've proof e-nough of your roy-al-ty. Let the wed-ding mu-sic play." And the peo-ple shout-ed qui-et-ly: "Hoo-ray!" For a

72 Tempo I°

prin - cess is a del - i - cate thing, Del - i - cate and dain - ty as a

dra - gon fly's wing. You can re - cog - nize a la - dy by her el - e - gant air, But a

Slowly

81

gen - u - ine prin - cess is ex - ceed - ing - ly rare.

Repeat ad lib.

- - fade out as curtain rises.

No. 3

Opening For A Princess

Cue: QUEEN: Now, don't dilly-dally, Dauntless. It's nearly time for your cocoa.

o-pen-ing for a prin-cess, For a gen-u-ine cer-ti-fied

LADIES: prin-cess. Tell us when you in-tend to end this di-lem-ma we're

KNIGHTS: in. None of the la-dies give a fig for liv-in' in

ALL: sin! We have an o-pen-ing for a prin-cess, For a

No. 4

In A Little While

ev - er hand in glove is the way I have it planned. But I'll

on - ly stay in love If the glove con-tains your hand.

I can see it all, Down to ev-'ry small de - tail. So I wish you'd

look a-round Un-til you've found a cas-tle in the neigh-bor-hood for sale.

(non rit.)

Tutti

p

(Dim out pit lights)

No. 5

In A Little While—Reprise

Cue: LARKEN: I believe you.

way I have it planned. But I'll on - ly stay in love If the

23 BOTH:

glove con-tains your hand. In a vel-vet gown {I'll / you'll} be com-ing down the

Col. 8va

+Ob. 8va

+Br. Hp.

aisle. And it's bound to seem as tho' the wait-ing's on - ly

Fl. Ob. Ob., Tpt.

Hp.

(H)

been a lit-tle, In a lit-tle while.

(L)

rit.

Col. 8va

a tempo

No. 6

Shy

cue: WINNIFRED: Anyway, here I am. Who's the lucky man?

And you may be sure: _____ way down deep I'm de-
mure. _____ Though some peo-ple I know might de-ny it, At
bot-tom I'm qui-et and pure! _____ I'm a-ware that it's
wrong _____ to be meek as I am; My chanc-es may pass me by. I pre-tend to be

strong ___ but as weak as I am, All I can do is try, God knows I

try! ___ Though I'm fright-ened and shy ___

___ And de-spite the im-pres-sion I give, I con-fess that I'm liv-ing a

lie, ___ Be-cause I'm ac-tual-ly ter-ri-bly ti-mid and hor-ri-bly

like-ly to fall on her face ———— When she's fi-nal-ly face to face with a pair of pants. Quite oft-en the la-dy's not as hard to please as she seems. ———— Quite

WINNIFRED:

brook. But how much long-er must I wait   With bait - ed

breath and ho - ok?

No. 6a

Fanfare

cue: QUEEN: When you marry - if you marry - - you'll marry a real princess, you'll - - -

No. 6b

The Minstrel, The Jester And I

cue: MINSTREL: We know you can't talk - - *(Dialogue continues)*

JESTER: You certainly do.
MINSTREL and JESTER:

voice in dis - guise. _____ You'll be hear - ing a tri - o and

not a du - et If you lis - ten with both of your eyes.

Kind - ly (lis - ten) with both of your (eyes.) _____ We pro -

duce a u - nique and re - mark - a - ble blend When we raise our three

+Tpts., Vib.

Hp.

Trb., Vla.

Solo Trb.

W. W., Hp., Str. pizz.

* In pantomime

No. 7   Sensitivity

lite. Com - mon peo - ple don't know what Ex - quis - ite a - gon -

y is, suf - fered by gen - tle peo - ple like me! Just

get your hands off me. Think up a trick - y test for that wretch - ed

moat swim - ming prin - cess. Ma - dame, may I sug - gest

WIZARD:

56

No. 8   The Swamps Of Home

cue: WINNIFRED: Well, I don't like to brag.

No. 9

Fight-Fight

cue: LARKEN: I hate you!

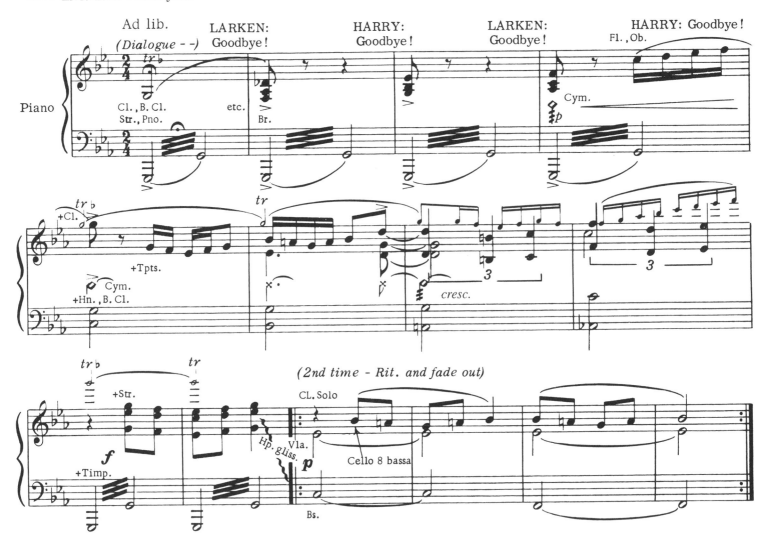

No. 10

Spanish Panic

cue: QUEEN: Why don't we all watch while court dancers Sir Harold and Lady Beatrice demonstrate?

QUEEN: Prepare - é

No. 11

Tents

No. 12

Normandy

cue:LARKEN: Quicksand?

Con Moto (In 2)

MINSTREL: It's April, isn't it? LARKEN: April?

No. 13

Spanish Panic No. 2

JESTER: You'd better not let the Queen catch you walking.

No. 14

Song of Love

cue: WINNIFRED: You can call me by my nickname.

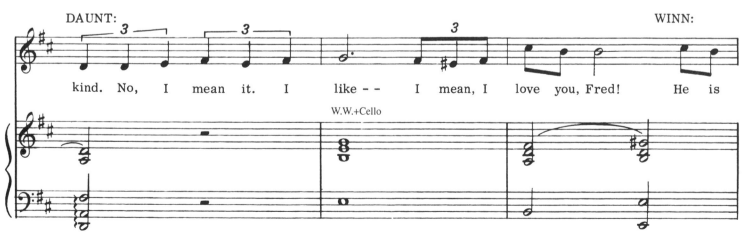

sing a mer-ry drink-ing song And let the wine be poured.

45 CHORUS:

Fill the bowl to o - ver flow-ing. Raise the gob-let high. With an

F and an R and an E and a D, And an F R E D, FRED, Yea! I'm in

DAUNT:

53

love with a girl named Fred. She sings just like a bird. You'll be

173 ALL:

Bra - vo, bra - vo, bra - vis - si - mo, Bra - vo,_____ bra - vis - si - mo,

177 *(handclaps)*

W.Blk.

WINN: *(completely wild, alcoholic abandon)*

185 CHORUS:

Ah ah ah, ah, ah, ah, ah, ah, ahhh!   Fill the bowl to o - ver - flow - ing,

Raise the gob - let high.   With an F and an R and an E and a D And an

End Act I

No. 15

Entr'acte

No. 16

Opening-Act II

cue: *LARKEN sneezes*

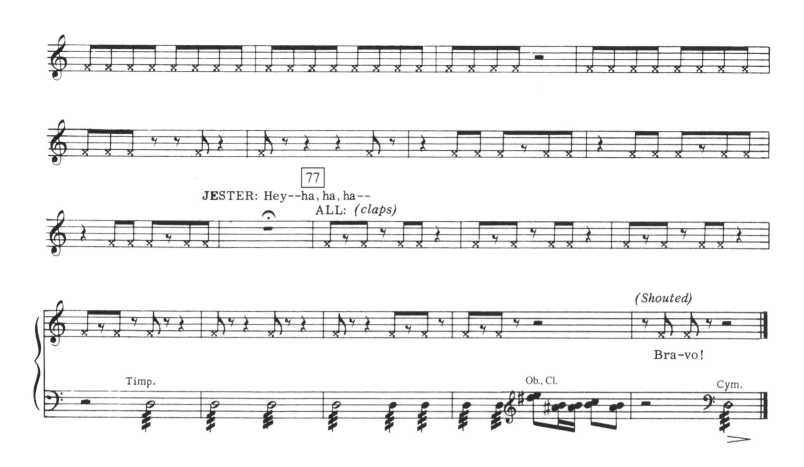

No. 17   Happily Ever After

cue: WINNIFRED picks up book and begins to read:

happily, happily, happily ever after. ___ The couple is

happily leaving the chapel eternally tied. As the

curtain descends there is nothing but loving and laughter. When the

fairy tale ends, the heroine's always a bride.

El - la, the girl of the cin - ders, __ Did the wash and the walls and the win - ders. __ But she

land - ed a prince who was brawn - y and blue - eyed and blond.

Still I hon - est - ly doubt that __ she could ev - er have done it with - out that __ Cra - zy

la - dy with the wand.

I have no one but me. __ Fair - y

(Spoken: Cinderella had outside help!)

(Spoken:) I haven't got a Fairy Godmother - - etc.

God-moth-er, God-moth-er, God-moth-er, Where can you be?

Snow -

white was so pret-ty, they tell us ____ That the queen was in-sult-ed and jeal-ous ____ When the

mir-ror de-clared that Snow-white was the fair-est of all.

She was dumped on the bor - der ___ But was saved by some men who a - dored her. ___ Oh, I

(Spoken:) But there were seven
of them, practically a regiment!

grant you— they were small. I'm a - lone in the night, ___ By my -

(Spoken:) That girl had seven etc. ...

self. Not a dwarf, not an elf, not a gob - lin in sight!

poison apple, even so —

She lived hap-pi-ly, hap-pi-ly, hap-pi-ly ev - er

af - ter. ___ A mag-i-cal kiss coun-ter-act-ed the ap-ple e-ven-tu-al -

ly. Though I know I'm not clev-er, I'll do what they tell me I haf-ta! I want some

hap-pi-ly ev - er af-ter to hap-pen to me. Ra -

fin-ished be-fore I be-gin _____ And be-sides I don't want to get out — I want to get

in! _____ 3 I want to live hap-pi-ly, hap-pi-ly, hap-pi-ly ev - er

af - ter. I want to walk hap-pi-ly out of a chap-el e-ter-nal-ly

tied. For I know that I'll nev-er live hap-pi-ly ev-er

No. 18 # Man To Man Talk

JESTER: Do your duty, Sire.

flow - er, boy flow - er, girl flow - er, Oh, tell me more, I

want to know a - bout what get - ting mar-ried is for.

fall from girl flow-er and

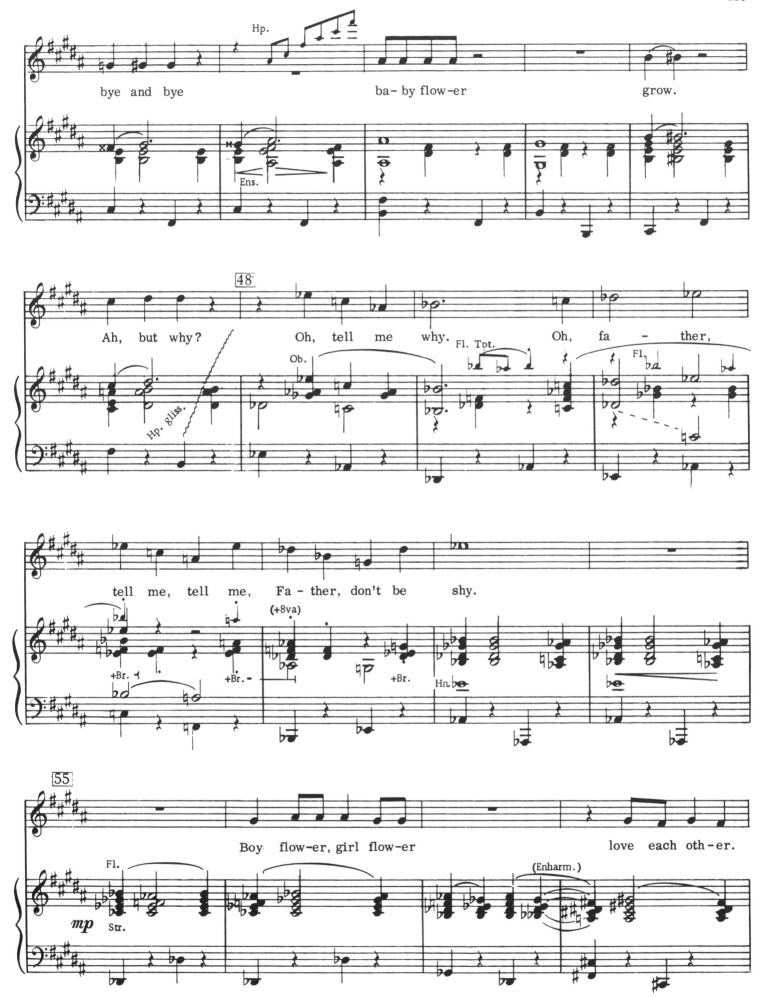

122

will get mar-ried-- and then--

One night-- *(Stork pantomime)*

Cue to continue:
DAUNTLESS: No, wait a minute, father.

Flow - er, seed, man, wom - an, bee, ba - by, small-- It

No. 19

Very Soft Shoes

Cue: *WIZARD goes up steps - (lights fade)*

crowd and the crown The crowd went cra - zy and the house came down When

Dad-dy wore his Ver-y soft ssh _____ oes.

Cls.
p

pp

Hp.

attacca

Three O'clock In The Morning

Slowly - in 4

Chime

Piano

p Str.

Vla.

Cello

+Vlns. 8va

Hp. o o o o   o o o o

R. H.

No. 21

Yesterday I Loved You

Cue: HARRY: Well, in a way I have.

more. _____ My

[17] heart can - not be trust - ed, _____ I

give you _____ fair warn - ing, _____ I

[25] Freely
o - pen - ly con - fess: _____ To - night I love you

138

must have been ut - ter - ly blind, _____ Or

else I was out of my mind _____ For I

113

find you so much love - li - er to -

LARKEN:

day. _____ My

heart can - not be trust - ed. _____ I

give you _____ fair warn - ing _____ For

HARRY:

129 In 4
(HARRY:)

Yes - ter - day I loved you, as nev - er be - fore. But

LARKEN:

In a lit - tle while, Just a lit - tle while, You and I will be One, two, three, four.

Hp.

+ Str., Pno.

Cello

Bs.

That was long a - go, And now it's best you know That to-

In a lit - tle while I will see you smile On the face of my son - to - be, For-

137 In 2

+ Fls., Vlns.

day _____ I love you e - ven

ev - er hand in glove _____ Is the

Br. (Ob., Cl. sust.)
Vla., Hn.
Hp.

more. _____ My

way I have it planned. _____ My

W. W., col. 8va

morn - ing.

No. 22   Nightingale Lullaby

Two starts

(First time)-*Cue*: QUEEN: You were brought here to put a live princess to sleep,
                     not to wake up a dead one.

(Second time-start at   ) *Cue*: WINNIFRED: Alright, we'll take it from the top.

No. 22a

Wizard

Cue: WINNIFRED: All right, sheep- - I'm ready when you are!

No. 23

Finale

Cue: KING: Hop!
Skip!

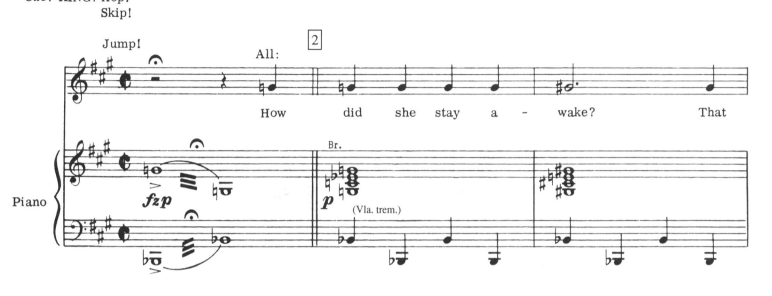

How did she stay a - wake? That

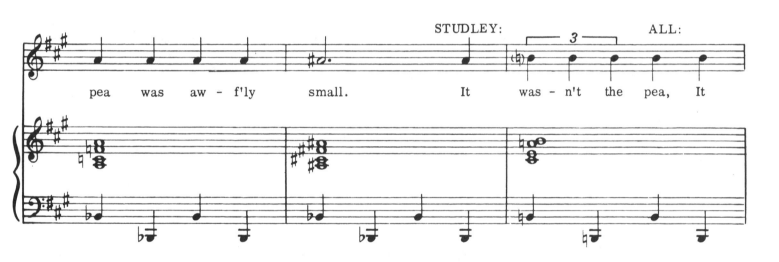

pea was aw - f'ly small. It was - n't the pea, It

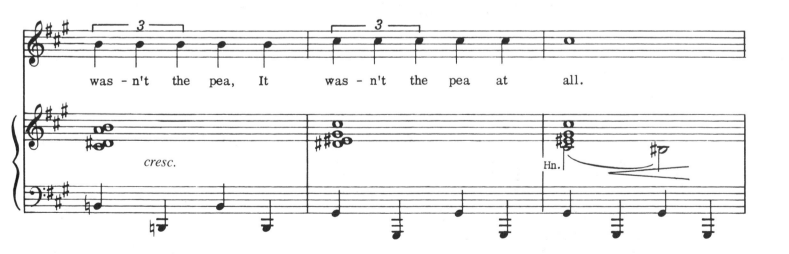

was - n't the pea, It was - n't the pea at all.

End Act II
attacca

No. 24 : Bows & Exit Music